BinaryCoder X

Coding essentials

"Unlock the language of innovation, where each line of code is a brushstroke on the canvas of possibility. Join me, BinaryCoder X, as we delve into the essentials and discover the transformative power of coding apps – a journey where creativity meets logic, and the digital landscape becomes your canvas."

BinaryCoder X

Contents

1.

2.

3.

4.

5.

6.

7.

8.

9.

10.

11.

12.

13.

14.

15.

16.

17.

18.

19.

20.

21.

22.

23.

Foreword

Foreword: Coding Essentials and Apps for Coding

In the vast realm of coding, where ones and zeros converge to shape the digital world, we find ourselves on an ever-accelerating journey of innovation and discovery. As we stand at the intersection of creativity and technology, "Coding Essentials and Apps for Coding" emerges as a guiding beacon in the hands of BinaryCoder X, your fellow explorer in this captivating universe.

In these pages, BinaryCoder X intricately weaves a narrative that transcends the syntax and semantics of code, unveiling the principles that underscore true mastery. From the essence of choosing the right language to the art of collaborating on real projects, each insight shared is a testament to the passion and dedication that fuels a coder's soul.

But this journey isn't confined to the desktop or the confines of a traditional coding space. BinaryCoder X propels us into the future, showcasing a curated selection of apps that seamlessly integrate coding into the fabric of our mobile lives. These apps redefine convenience, transforming your smartphone into a dynamic coding companion that empowers you to learn, practice, and collaborate at your own pace.

As you embark on this expedition, guided by BinaryCoder X's wealth of experience and enthusiasm for the craft, remember that coding is more than a skill; it's a language through which ideas come to life, solutions emerge, and the digital landscape evolves. "Coding Essentials and Apps for Coding" is not just a guide; it's an invitation to explore the boundless possibilities that coding offers.

May this foreword ignite your curiosity, fuel your passion, and set the stage for a journey that transcends the binary, unlocking the true essence of coding mastery. Welcome to a world where BinaryCoder X invites you to not just decipher the code but to embrace the beauty, creativity, and infinite potential that coding holds.

Preface

Preface: Coding Essentials and Apps for Coding

Welcome to the dynamic universe of coding, where creativity meets logic, and possibilities are limitless. "Coding Essentials and Apps for Coding" serves as your compass in navigating the intricacies of this ever-evolving landscape. Whether you're a budding enthusiast embarking on your coding journey or a seasoned developer seeking to expand your toolkit, this guide is crafted to be your trusted companion.

In the pages ahead, we unravel the fundamental principles that lay the foundation for coding mastery. From setting clear goals to continuous learning, each chapter is a stepping stone toward honing your skills and embracing the art of coding. Delve into the essence of choosing the right language, understanding the basics, and engaging in real projects — each lesson designed to empower you with practical knowledge.

But the journey doesn't end there. In the digital era, where mobility is paramount, we explore a curated selection of apps that transcend traditional boundaries. These apps transform your mobile device into a powerhouse for coding education and practice. Whether you're refining your Python skills on the go or collaborating with a global coding community, these apps bring coding to your fingertips, anytime, anywhere.

As you embark on this odyssey through coding essentials and discover the transformative potential of coding apps, remember: coding is not just about writing lines of code; it's a journey of exploration, problem-solving, and continuous growth. Let this guide be your compass, and may your coding endeavors be as boundless as the world of possibilities that coding unfolds before you. Welcome to the adventure of coding essentials and the innovative realm of coding apps.

Acknowledgement

Acknowledgment: Coding Essentials and Apps for Coding

In the vast tapestry of coding, where every line of code weaves a story, I stand humbled and grateful, surrounded by the collective spirit of the coding community. "Coding Essentials and Apps for Coding" has been a labor of love, and its creation wouldn't have been possible without the support, encouragement, and inspiration from remarkable individuals and resources.

To the coding community, whose collective wisdom and passion for innovation fuel the ever-evolving landscape of coding, I extend my heartfelt gratitude. Your contributions to the world of open source, forums, and collaborative projects are the driving force behind the principles outlined in this guide.

A special acknowledgment to mentors and educators who have shared their knowledge generously, guiding countless coding enthusiasts on their learning journeys. Your commitment to nurturing the next generation of coders is a beacon of inspiration.

To fellow coders who tirelessly experiment, solve problems, and push the boundaries of what's possible – you are the heartbeat of this vibrant ecosystem. Your dedication to the craft is the foundation upon which "Coding Essentials and Apps for Coding" stands.

I express deep appreciation to the developers and creators behind the coding apps featured in this guide. Your innovation has transformed mobile devices into powerful coding tools, enabling learners and professionals alike to carry the spirit of coding wherever they go.

Last but not least, to readers – aspiring coders, seasoned developers, and everyone in between – thank you for embarking on this coding journey with me. May the pages ahead inspire, challenge, and empower you to explore the boundless realms of coding.

In the spirit of continuous learning and collaboration, let's continue to code, create, and push the boundaries of what's possible.

BinaryCoder   X

1

Apps For Coding

Certainly! Here are 10 more apps for coding:

1. Juno Wallet:

- An app that allows you to earn rewards by participating in coding challenges and competitions.

2. VimTouch:

- A mobile version of the popular Vim text editor, providing a powerful coding environment for those familiar with Vim.

3. Coda:

- A mobile code editor supporting syntax highlighting for various programming languages.

4. JupyterLab:

- An interactive development environment for Jupyter Notebooks, providing a flexible and extensible coding environment.

5. Termux:

- A powerful terminal emulator for Android that enables you to run Linux commands and use various programming tools.

6. Pythonista:

- An iOS app for Python programming, offering a Python IDE with features like code editing, debugging, and automation.

7. AIDE Web - HTML, CSS, JavaScript:

- An Android app for web development, supporting HTML, CSS, and JavaScript coding with a built-in editor and preview features.

8. Dcoder, Compiler IDE:

- A mobile coding IDE supporting a wide range of programming languages, with coding challenges and a compiler.

9. Juno Connect:

- An app that complements Jupyter Notebooks, providing a remote interface for accessing and running Jupyter notebooks.

10. Dcoder, Compiler IDE (iOS):

- The iOS version of Dcoder, offering a mobile coding IDE for various programming languages.

2

Set Clear Goals

Set Clear Goals:

Before diving into coding, establish clear and achievable goals. Define what you want to achieve with your coding journey—whether it's building a website, developing a mobile app, or mastering a specific programming language. Having well-defined goals provides direction, motivation, and a roadmap for your learning path. It helps you stay focused, measure progress, and tailor your coding activities to align with your aspirations. Whether you aim to become a web developer, data scientist, or software engineer, knowing your goals is the first step in creating a purposeful and effective coding experience.

3

Choose the Right Language:

Choose the Right Language:

Selecting the appropriate programming language is crucial in shaping your coding journey. Different languages serve various purposes, from web development (e.g., HTML, CSS, JavaScript) to data science (e.g., Python, R) or systems programming (e.g., C, C++). Consider your goals and the type of projects you envision working on. If you're a beginner, languages with clear syntax and extensive community support, like Python, may be a good starting point. Research and understand the strengths of each language to make an informed decision that aligns with your coding objectives. Choosing the right language lays the foundation for a rewarding and efficient coding experience.

4

Understand the Basics:

U nderstand the Basics:

To build a strong coding foundation, focus on mastering the fundamental concepts of programming. Ensure a solid understanding of variables, data types, loops, conditionals, and functions. These basics serve as the building blocks for more complex coding tasks. Familiarity with these concepts not only enhances your problem-solving abilities but also makes it easier to grasp advanced topics as you progress in your coding journey. Invest time in thoroughly understanding the basics, as they are the scaffolding upon which your coding expertise will be constructed.

5

Practice Regularly

Practice Regularly:

Consistent and deliberate practice is key to becoming proficient in coding. Allocate dedicated time regularly to write code, solve problems, and work on projects. Regular practice helps reinforce your understanding of coding concepts, improves your problem-solving skills, and builds muscle memory in terms of syntax and structure. Set aside specific periods in your schedule for coding sessions, and make it a routine. The more you code, the more comfortable and confident you'll become, accelerating your learning process and enhancing your overall coding abilities.

6

Use Online Resources

Use Online Resources:

Take advantage of the wealth of online resources available for learning and improving coding skills. Platforms like Codecademy, freeCodeCamp, and Khan Academy offer interactive lessons, exercises, and projects. Explore coding forums such as Stack Overflow for problem-solving and discussions. Utilize documentation for programming languages and frameworks. Online resources provide diverse learning opportunities, from structured courses to real-world problem-solving, making them invaluable for both beginners and experienced coders seeking to enhance their skills and stay updated with the latest developments in the coding landscape.

7

Work on Real Projects

Work on Real Projects:

Transcend theoretical knowledge by engaging in real-world coding projects. Apply the skills you've learned to practical scenarios, whether it's developing a personal website, building a small application, or contributing to an open-source project. Real projects provide hands-on experience, presenting challenges that require problem-solving and decision-making. They not only solidify your understanding of coding concepts but also showcase your abilities to potential employers. By working on tangible projects, you gain valuable insights into the coding process, from planning and implementation to debugging and optimization, fostering a deeper and more practical understanding of coding.

8

Learn Version Control

Learn Version Control:

Understanding version control, especially with tools like Git, is essential for effective collaboration and code management. Version control allows you to track changes in your code, collaborate seamlessly with others, and revert to previous versions if needed. Familiarize yourself with basic Git commands, repositories, and branching strategies. Platforms like GitHub and Bitbucket complement version control systems, providing a collaborative environment for sharing code and working on projects with teams. Incorporating version control into your coding workflow enhances efficiency, promotes collaboration, and instills good practices in managing code throughout your coding journey.

9

Read Code

Read Code:

Expand your coding proficiency by actively reading code written by others. Delve into open-source projects, GitHub repositories, or community forums to explore diverse coding styles, techniques, and best practices. Reading code written by experienced developers exposes you to different approaches to problem-solving, coding conventions, and effective strategies for writing clean and maintainable code. Analyzing code helps improve your comprehension skills, allows you to learn from real-world examples, and provides insights into the broader coding community. Make it a habit to study and understand various codebases, as it contributes significantly to your growth as a proficient coder.

10

Ask for Feedback

Ask for Feedback:

Seeking and receiving constructive feedback on your code is a crucial step in the learning process. Share your work with peers, mentors, or online communities and invite input on your coding style, structure, and logic. Constructive feedback provides valuable insights into areas of improvement, alternative solutions, and best practices. Embrace the feedback loop as an opportunity for growth, and use it to refine your coding skills. This iterative process not only enhances the quality of your code but also accelerates your learning journey by exposing you to diverse perspectives and coding approaches.

11

Attend Coding Meetups

Attend Coding Meetups:

Immerse yourself in the coding community by attending local or virtual coding meetups. These gatherings provide opportunities to connect with fellow coders, share experiences, and learn from others in a collaborative setting. Attendees often discuss coding trends, share insights, and even collaborate on projects. Coding meetups not only foster a sense of community but also expose you to diverse perspectives and approaches to coding. Engaging with like-minded individuals enhances networking, provides support, and creates a supportive environment for continuous learning throughout your coding journey.

12

Master Debugging

Master Debugging:

Developing effective debugging skills is essential for every coder. Learn to identify and fix errors in your code systematically. Familiarize yourself with debugging tools provided by your programming environment and cultivate a methodical approach to troubleshooting. Understanding error messages, using breakpoints, and stepping through code are valuable techniques. Debugging not only resolves issues but also deepens your understanding of how code executes. As you master this skill, you'll become more adept at handling complex coding challenges and ensuring the reliability of your programs.

13

Explore Data Structures and Algorithms

Explore Data Structures and Algorithms:

Dive into the world of data structures and algorithms to strengthen your problem-solving abilities. Understand the fundamentals of data structures such as arrays, linked lists, and trees, as well as algorithms like sorting and searching. Knowledge in this area is crucial for writing efficient and optimized code. Explore algorithmic patterns, study their time and space complexities, and practice solving algorithmic challenges on platforms like LeetCode or HackerRank. A solid foundation in data structures and algorithms empowers you to tackle a wide range of coding problems and enhances your overall coding prowess.

14

Document Your Code

Document Your Code:

Cultivate the habit of good code documentation. Clearly articulate the purpose, functionality, and usage of your code through comments and documentation. Documentation serves as a guide for others (and your future self) to understand and work with your code. It enhances collaboration within teams and contributes to the maintainability of your projects. Adopt a consistent and meaningful commenting style, explaining complex sections and the rationale behind your code. Effective documentation is a hallmark of professional coding, emphasizing clarity and transparency in your programming endeavors.

15

Follow Coding Standards

Follow Coding Standards:

Adhering to coding standards is crucial for writing clean, readable, and maintainable code. Familiarize yourself with the coding conventions specific to the programming languages you use. Consistent indentation, naming conventions, and code structure not only improve code readability but also facilitate collaboration within development teams. Many programming languages have established style guides, such as PEP 8 for Python or Google's Java Style Guide, which provide recommendations on coding best practices. By following coding standards, you contribute to a more uniform and efficient coding environment, making your code more accessible and understandable to others.

16

Engage in Pair Programming

Engage in Pair Programming:

Pair programming is a collaborative coding technique where two individuals work together on the same piece of code. One person writes the code (the driver), while the other reviews each line in real-time (the observer). Roles can be swapped regularly. This practice fosters effective communication, knowledge sharing, and problem-solving. Pair programming not only enhances the quality of code through immediate feedback but also accelerates learning as both individuals contribute their insights and expertise. Consider incorporating pair programming into your coding routine, whether working with a colleague or collaborator online, to leverage the collective strengths of a coding partnership.

17

Stay Updated

Stay Updated:

The field of coding is dynamic, with new technologies, frameworks, and best practices emerging regularly. Stay informed by actively seeking updates on industry trends, advancements, and changes in coding languages. Follow reputable blogs, subscribe to coding newsletters, and engage with online communities to stay abreast of the latest developments. Continuous learning is fundamental in coding, and staying updated ensures that your skills remain relevant and adaptable to the evolving landscape. Attend webinars, conferences, or workshops to gain insights from experts and connect with the broader coding community. Embrace a mindset of lifelong learning to thrive in the ever-changing world of coding.

18

Participate in Coding Challenges

Participate in Coding Challenges:

Engage in coding challenges on platforms like HackerRank, LeetCode, or CodeWars to sharpen your problem-solving skills. These challenges present diverse coding scenarios and algorithmic puzzles that test your ability to devise efficient solutions. Regular participation not only hones your coding proficiency but also exposes you to a variety of problem-solving approaches. Overcoming coding challenges builds resilience, creativity, and adaptability, essential qualities for any coder. Embrace the opportunity to tackle new problems regularly, fostering a mindset that welcomes challenges as valuable learning experiences in your coding journey.

19

Build a Portfolio

Build a Portfolio:

Constructing a coding portfolio is more than a showcase; it's a testament to your skills and accomplishments. Compile and present your completed projects, highlighting the technologies, challenges, and outcomes. A portfolio provides a tangible representation of your coding journey, offering potential employers or collaborators insight into your capabilities. It becomes a living document that evolves with your skills, demonstrating growth and a diverse range of coding experiences. Ensure your portfolio includes project descriptions, code snippets, and links to live projects or repositories. A well-crafted portfolio not only sets you apart but serves as a comprehensive record of your coding achievements.

20

Join Open Source Projects

J oin Open Source Projects:

Contribute to open source projects to gain practical experience and collaborate with a wider coding community. Open source projects provide opportunities to work on real-world applications, learn from experienced developers, and contribute to software that impacts users globally. Participating in open source development enhances your coding skills, exposes you to industry-standard practices, and allows you to build a diverse portfolio. Platforms like GitHub host a myriad of open source projects across various domains, providing ample opportunities for developers at all skill levels to make meaningful contributions. Joining open source projects is not just about code; it's about collaboration, learning, and making a positive impact on the coding   community.

21

Never Stop Learning

Never Stop Learning:

Embrace a mindset of continuous learning throughout your coding journey. The field of coding evolves rapidly, introducing new languages, frameworks, and methodologies. Stay curious, explore emerging technologies, and be open to expanding your skill set. Engage with online courses, attend workshops, and read industry publications to stay informed about the latest advancements. Networking with other coders, participating in coding events, and seeking mentorship contribute to your growth. Recognize that learning is a lifelong process, and each coding challenge, project, or interaction is an opportunity to deepen your knowledge and expertise. In the ever-evolving world of coding, the passion for learning is the key to sustained success.